NATURE

Elizabeth James

Colour Me Calm Book 1

First published in 2015 by Kyle Craig Publishing

Copyright © 2015 Kyle Craig Publishing

Design: Elizabeth James, Julie Anson, Alison McNicol, Shutterstock, Inc.

ISBN: 978-1-78595-084-1

A CIP record for this book is available from the British Library.

A Kyle Craig Publication

www.kyle-craig.com

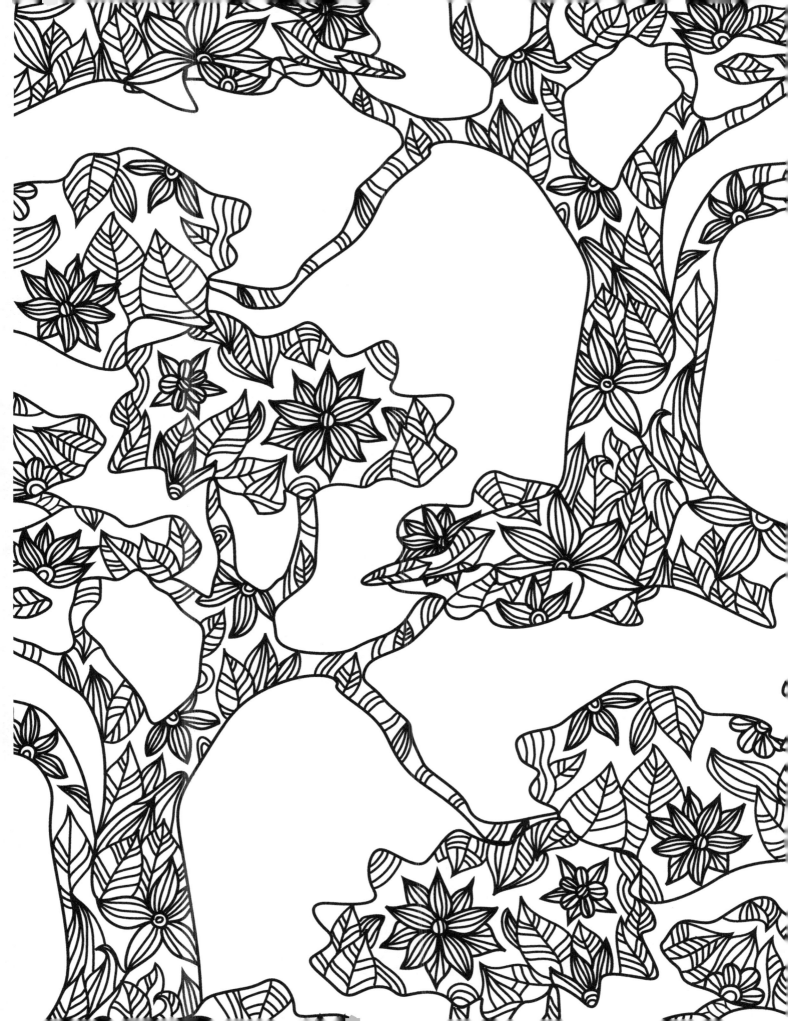

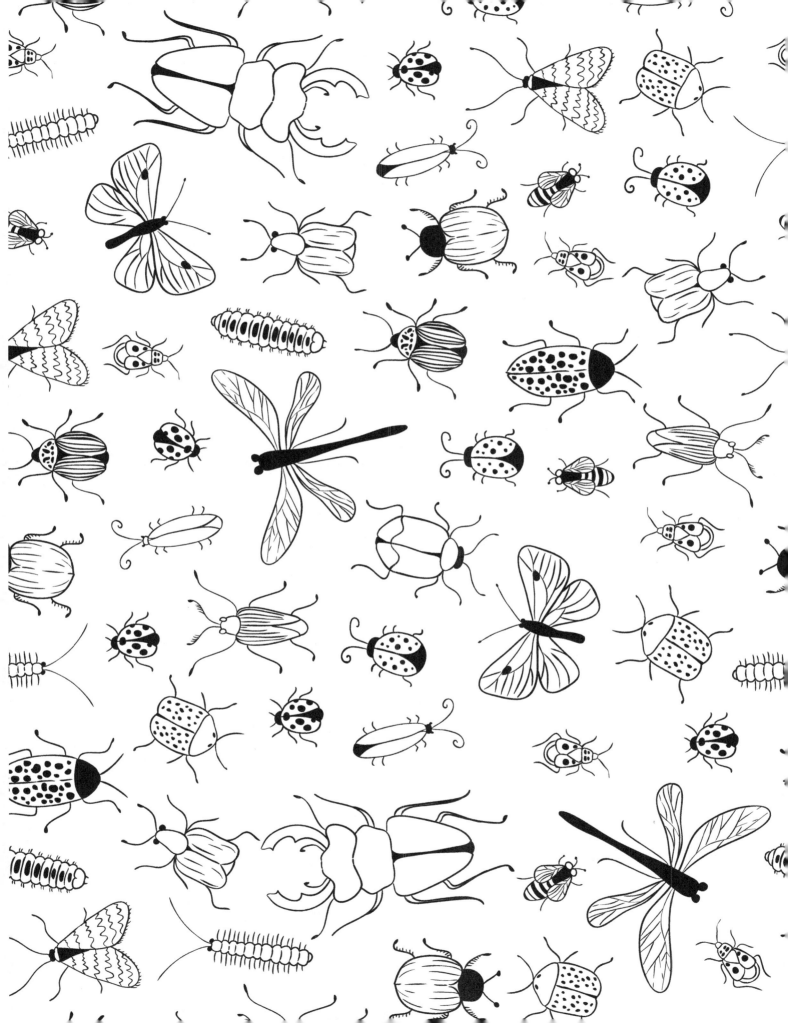

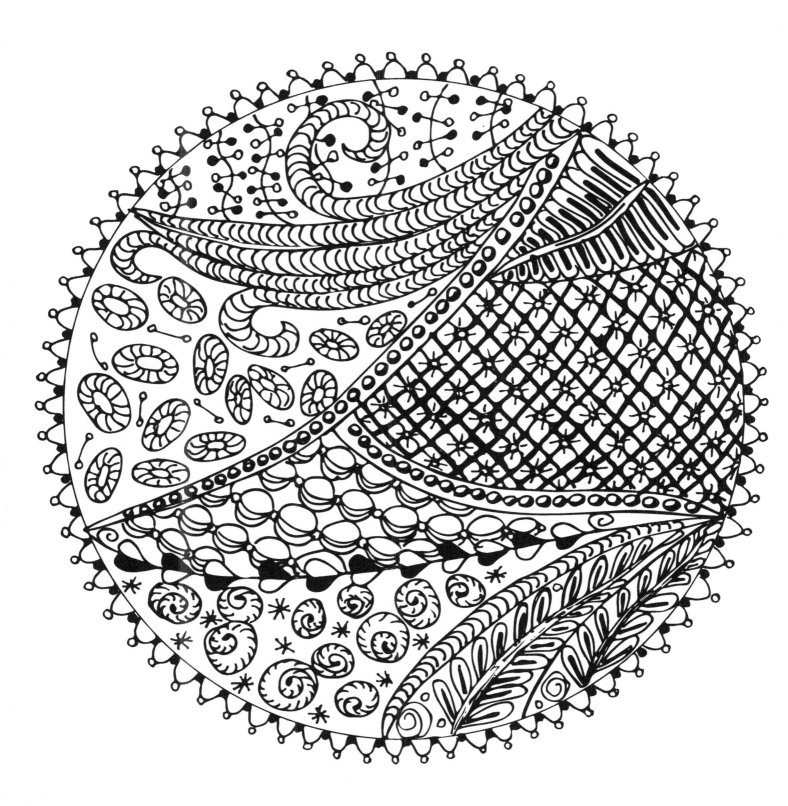

Made in the USA
Las Vegas, NV
08 December 2021